BRIGHT TOMORROWS

Poems of Hope and Inspiration

BRIGHT TOMORROWS

Poems of Hope and Inspiration

Phyllis C. Michael

Photography by Bill Engel

Fleming H. Revell Company
Old Tappan, New Jersey

Library of Congress Cataloging-in-Publication Data

Michael, Phyllis C.
  Bright tomorrows.

  1. Christian poetry, American. I. Title.
PS3563.I26B7 1989   811'.54   89-4031
ISBN 0-8007-1617-5

To you,
Dad,
for you taught me
faith, hope,
Christian love,
and courage—
the kind that holds on
stronger and longer
when north winds blow.

CONTENTS

Trust

Hope

Promise

PREFACE

Is there anyone anywhere whose daily blessings haven't at some time become scrambled with disappointments, heartaches, and failures? Perhaps at this very moment your own frustrations are catapulting over one another like angry hornets whose nest has been disturbed. As for me, some days are so chock-full of blighted hopes that I wouldn't see a rainbow even if it stayed put for hours right outside my front door.

Often, too, I've created my own disappointments by trying to climb to the moon by hanging on to a gossamer spiderweb. And I've blamed God for everything from mud tracks on my floor to knots in my shoestrings. But I am learning. God doesn't push me off the cliff if I carelessly get too close to the edge. Oh, yes, I just might tumble off because of my poor judgment. And crush my exalted opinion of myself on the rock ledge below. . . splatter my faith like a bucket of paint. In which case, how can I blame God?

Through the years I have come to know that in spite of appearances at times, God *does* care. And although we may not understand His ways, the only true path to inner peace is the one marked Faith. We must accept what comes our way and say with Job: ". . . Yet will I trust in him. . ." (Job 13:15).

I can see the beauty of God's good earth, but I can't tie in a neat little package and weigh God's power, His wisdom, His eternal love, His grace and mercy. The breadth and scope of each is far too vast for my mind to perceive. And if I ever doubt or deny them, they aren't destroyed or even lessened one little bit. *They are! God is!*

God is! Then let's live each day *knowing* this. Let's share our faith, our joy in this knowledge. He walks with us. His comfort is there for us. Surely goodness and mercy, His goodness and mercy, are ours for now and for eternity.

Phyllis C. Michael

BRIGHT TOMORROWS

Poems of Hope and Inspiration

GRATITUDE

The Lord is my shepherd; I shall not want.
He maketh me to lie down in green pastures:
he leadeth me beside the still waters.

Psalms 23:1,2

Thanks Be to God

Oh, what a marvelous place is God's earth!
Words can't express the half of its worth;
Tongues cannot tell all the beauty I see,
Oh, how God loves, He loves even me!

Oh, what a foretaste of glory divine
Just to recall each blessing that's mine;
Though I am weak and unworthy indeed,
God in His love supplies every need.

Life everlasting is part of God's plan,
What greater gift could be given to man?
Oh, how my heart and my whole being sings,
"Thanks be to God, the King of all Kings.
                    Thanks be to God!
                    Thanks be to God!
Thanks be to God for each gift from above,
Thanks be to God for His wonderful love."

. . . O Lord my God, I will give thanks unto thee for ever.

Psalms 30:12

Oh, the Wonder!

The earth declares its Maker's praise
    In, oh, so many different ways;
It speaks in daytime colors bright
    And in the stillness of the night;
Each realm of space reveals God's voice,
    Each star appears by His own choice;
The sun, the moon, the planets, too,
    Each move just like He planned they'd do.

The sea obeys the Master's will;
    He says, "Roll on!" or "Peace, be still!"
Both wind and wave heed His commands,
    Both time and tide are in His hands.
Then who am I that I should fail
    To trust when storms of life prevail?
Give thanks, my soul, in *everything*;
    Rejoice! Rejoice! Give thanks and sing.
Oh, the wonder of God's vast domain,
    The earth, the sea, the sky!
Oh, the fullness of His matchless love
    To care for such as I!

. . . yes, praise the Lord! Sing him a new song. Sing his praises,
all his people.

Psalms 149:1 TLB

Make Me Aware

I do not ask for greener grass
Or skies of deeper blue;
I do not ask for smoother paths
Or wider view.

I only ask, Lord, let my heart
Give thanks for things that are;
Let grateful eyes see light in each
Small star.

I do not ask for sweeter songs
But just for ears that hear
The symphony of your great love
In all things far and near.

I only ask to touch a rose
And feel your tender care;
I only ask, Lord, by Thy grace,
Make me—aware.

If any of you lack wisdom, let him ask of God. . . .

James 1:5

How Rich Am I!

What use are things of earth and such?
   They rust or melt away;
Then as for me I'll serve the Lord,
   His love will not decay.
How rich am I! I'll sing God's praise
   Nor fear what man can do;
I have true wealth, God's perfect peace,
   All this and heaven, too.

What use is gold when hope is lost?
   Some things gold cannot buy;
Then as for me I'll serve the Lord,
   Each need He shall supply.
Could joy be counted just like gold,
   I'd be a millionaire;
My heart o'erflows with happiness,
   I'm safe within God's care.

But seek ye first the kingdom of God, and his righteousness;
and all these things shall be added unto you.

Matthew 6:33

I Watched a Miracle

I watched the dawn come shining through
This morning on my knees;
I saw the darkness change to light
As quickly as you please;
I saw the miracle of God
Before my very eyes;
How great God is, how good God is!
How wondrous and how wise!

I saw the twilight come again,
The sun sink out of sight;
And o'er the waiting earth came peace,
'Twas wrapped in softest night.
I know the dawn will come again
Tomorrow when I wake;
I watched a miracle tonight
That only God can make.

The earth is the Lord's, and the fulness thereof. . . .

Psalms 24:1

Miracles

The grandeur of a mountain peak,
   The vastness of the sea,
The very ground on which I stand,
   All these are proof to me—
      God is.

The tree that cradles leafy buds
   And stretches root and limb,
The rose whose pink unfolds and drinks
   The morning dew knows Him—
      God is.

The stars that jewel the darkest night,
   The clouds that scurry by,
The sun that warms us through and
    through
   All speak for earth and sky—
      God is.

A baby robin learns to sing
   Wheat seeds will sprout and grow,
A golden butterfly glides by,
   These miracles all show—
      God is.
A mighty power unseen unheard
   Rules all of time and tide;
I breathe, I hear, I talk, I walk,
   Ah, this can't be denied—
      God is.

Mere man can't make the thunder roar
   Or create a tiny ant,
A mammoth cave or a fish that swims,
   So each of us must grant—
      God is,
      God IS!

How great are his signs! and how mighty are his wonders. . . .

Daniel 4:3

FAITH

He restoreth my soul: he leadeth me in the paths of righteousness for his name's sake.

Psalms 23:3

Faith Is

Faith is
believing
seeing with one's mind
after the night
comes light.

Faith is
knowing
accepting
in one's heart and soul
summer with its flowers
follows spring showers.

Faith is
trusting
resting assured
in every nerve and cell
of one's body
God is there, *always* there,
here—everywhere.

*Then touched he their eyes, saying, According to your faith
be it unto you.*

Matthew 9:29

Biding God's Time

Roses and orchids each bloom in their season;
But then perhaps without knowing the reason
They rest.
Never wasting a moment in scolding or weeping
They patiently await in God's own tender keeping
The crest.
Their beauty lies deep within them hidden
Until the time it's softly bidden
To rise.
They need this quiet time to capture
Strength and all the perfect rapture
Which lies
In roots, in soil, in sun and rain.
Just so we, too, have much to gain
If we
With hearts filled with faith molded
    and still
Like buds, await God's perfect will
To be.

. . . let us run with patience the race that is set before us.

Hebrews 12:1

Not Mine to Ask

It is not mine to ask today
    Why this or that must be,
Why some dark cloud must hide the sun,
    Why pain should come to me.

It is but mine to say, "God is
    And somewhere in His plan
This, too, must have its rightful place
    Beyond the scope of man."

It is but mine to say, "Lead on,
    O precious Lord divine;
Some day I'll surely understand
    Take Thou my hand in Thine."

Preserve me, O God: for in thee do I put my trust.

Psalms 16:1

He's There

If there's a breeze, a worthy breeze,
  A kite can fly quite high;
Up, up above the earth it sails
  Wind anchored in the sky.

If there's a God, and there *is* a God,
  His arms won't let you fall;
They will sustain, they will give hope—
  He loves us, loves us—all.

Then trust in His unfailing power,
  Give Him your every care;
Lean back and rest upon His breast,
  He's there, He's *always* there.

Thou wilt keep him in perfect peace, whose mind is stayed on thee: because he trusteth in thee.

Isaiah 26:3

Remind Me, Lord

I sometimes get forgetful
    When comes a rainy day
That flowers need more than sunshine
    And I need time to pray.

The world whirls 'round about me
    And I whirl, too, I guess
Forgetting He who made me
    Wants only thus to bless.

If I must be reminded
    Or fail to understand,
Lord, whisper to me softly
    And please hold tight my hand.

Bless the Lord, O my soul, and forget not all his benefits.

Psalms 103:2

Step by Step

Lord, keep me climbing inch by inch
    Though mountains bar my way;
Yes, keep me walking step by step
    In faith all through the day.

For as I climb, Lord, this I know
    The path shall seem less steep;
Just keep me walking step by step
    Assured my watch You'll keep.

Lord, keep me climbing inch by inch
    Beyond my grief and care;
Yes, keep me walking step by step
    Aware that You are there.

You are there, yes, You are there
    And all Your plan unfolds
As I walk bravely step by step
    Toward what tomorrow holds.

The eternal God is your Refuge, And underneath are the everlasting arms. . . .

Deuteronomy 33:27 TLB

Faith Is the Thing

No man ever climbed to lofty heights
  By thinking he couldn't do it;
But he has slipped backward a step or two
  By simply saying, "I knew it!"

Yes, even an ant can carry a load
  Right over the ground or through it
Though it's twice his size, if he tells himself,
  "There's really nothing to it."

Faith is the thing one needs to rise
  Above one's own imperfection—
Faith in a God whose eyes are turned
  Just now in your direction.

Faith is the thing one needs to win,
  True faith and hope—never lose them;
With your hand in the Lord's, launch out
    in the deep;
  God gave you your talents—use them.

And let us not get tired of doing what is right, for after a while we will reap a harvest of blessing if we don't get discouraged and give up.

Galatians 6:9 TLB

PEACE

*Yea, though I walk through the valley of the
shadow of death, I will fear no evil: for thou
art with me; thy rod and thy staff they comfort me.*

Psalms 23:4

I Do Not Ask

I do not ask for bluer skies,
More days of summer sun,
But just the will to trust, dear Lord,
Thy wisdom in each one.
Not happier lark to greet the dawn
Or rose of sweeter smell,
But peace within this heart of mine,
Aware that all is well.

Not greener pasture, wider stream
To lie beside and rest
But hope that leads me step by step
Assured Thy way is best.
Not badge of power, not wings of fame
To flaunt fine art or skill,
But love that hears a rhapsody
Within Thy perfect will.

Not greater strength, but courage, Lord,
To rise when comes defeat;
Not greater joy, but greater faith
To share with those I meet.
Not golden treasure from Thy wealth,
More goodness from Thy hand,
But just the grace, please, to accept
Things I can't understand.

. . .*not my will, but thine, be done.*

Luke 22:42

Faith Answers

My soul has been tried
Yes a thousand times
In the fiery furnace
    of grief;
It's been tempered so often
By pain and by loss
That it cries out
    in disbelief,
"Peace, blessed peace,
There *is* no peace
This side the heavenly
    gates!"
But Faith answers, "Peace,
True peace *will* come
To him who trusts . . .
    and waits."

And the peace of God, which passeth all understanding, shall keep your hearts and minds through Christ Jesus.

Philippians 4:7

By Grace, Not Sight

I cannot see beyond today,
    Nor can I change God's plan;
I do not know what lies ahead
    But this I know—God can.
I see but one small patch of earth,
    God sees all time and space;
And this I know, whatever comes
    Sufficient is His grace.

How?

How could I know peace
    without tasting pain
Or revel in sunshine
    if we had no rain?
How could I sense daylight
    if we had no night?
Yes, God's in His heaven
    and the world is all right.

When thou passeth through the waters, I will be with thee. . . .

Isaiah 43:2

If I Should Choose

Of all the things I'm thankful for,
   If I could choose just one
To place above all other things
   When all is said and done,
I'd choose just this: My God is there
   In joy or yet in pain!
My God is there! He walks with me,
   Yes, even in the rain;
Not only when the roses bloom,
   Not only in the spring;
Not only when the world is gold,
   The sun on everything,
But *all* the time—God's *always*
there,
   He's with me day and night;
I cannot wander from His care
   Nor leave His precious sight.

Ah! God is there! Yes, God is there!
   What peace this brings to me!
I know, I know my God is *there*—
   My path I *need not*—see.

. . . he that keepeth thee will not slumber.

Psalms 121:3

In His Care

Life's road seems long and lonely at times
When heartaches come our way;
The night seems more than we can bear
Till coming of the day.

But keep in mind there's One who knows
And truly understands;
Just put your future in His care,
Just leave it in His hands.
He'll comfort you and give you peace
If you but trust His will.
Rest in this thought, He's always near,
His love is with you still.

Rest in the Lord, and wait patiently for him. . . .

Psalms 37:7

At Last

The day dawns clear and the sun
    shines bright
Erasing every trace of night;
It's happened time and time again
And that's the way it's always been.
So though the darkness seems to last,
Soon you will say, "This, too, has passed!"
Have faith in Him who holds earth's plans
Within His wise and loving hands;
Lean patiently upon His breast
And He will give you peace and rest.

He will keep in perfect peace all those who trust in him. . . .

Isaiah 26:3 TLB

HEARTACHES

*Thou preparest a table before me in the presence of
mine enemies. . . .*

Psalms 23:5

Trust and Pray On

Out of the depths of the wildest storm
Blue skies will come again;
Trust in the Lord, just trust and pray on,
His love will shine through the rain.

Faith has two eyes that look up to God,
Faith never doubts or fears;
Trust in the Lord, just trust and pray on
Until the storm disappears.

Faith has two ears that can hear God's will,
Faith puts your hand in His;
Trust in the Lord, just trust and pray on
For faith truly knows God is.

Faith has two arms that reach out toward God,
Faith has a heart of love;
Trust in the Lord, just trust and pray on
And help *will* come from above.

Is anyone among you suffering?
He should keep praying about it. . . .

James 5:13 TLB

All I Need To Know

Teach me, O Lord, to see Your love
In every drop of rain;
Teach me to feel Your presence near
Yes, even when there's pain.
Teach me to praise Your Name by faith
Whatever comes my way,
To know that midnight hours descend
Before the light of day.
Teach me acceptance, Lord, I ask,
Submission to Your will,
Not resignation but the grace
To seek Your wisdom still.
Teach me that wells sometimes run dry,
That rivers overflow
But You are always in control—
That's all I *need* to know.

Casting all your care upon him; for he careth for you.

1 Peter 5:7

Time Alone

Time alone cannot heal a wound,
   It takes a little prayer;
It takes true faith in God above—
   Just cast on Him your care.

Time alone cannot heal a wound
   For grief grows deeper still
As hours turn into days and years
   If *that* is what you will.

Time alone cannot heal a wound,
   You, too, must do your part;
It takes a smile upon your lips,
   True faith inside your heart.

*Why be discouraged and sad? Hope in God! I shall yet praise
him again. Yes, I shall again praise him for his help.*

Psalms 42:5 TLB

When Troubles Come

When troubles come as troubles do
To each of us—to me—to you,

It's not our task to ask God why;
It's ours to trust as days go by.

We cannot see beyond the crest
Of yonder hill, but God knows best;

In His all wise and loving way
He'll guide and guard us day by day.

Although you can't quite understand,
Just put your all in His dear hand;

He sees, He hears, He knows, He cares
About each burden *each* heart bears

And He'll send strength to meet this test;
Within His will securely rest.

. . . I will not fail thee, nor forsake thee.

Joshua 1:5

In Every Life

There comes a time in every life
  When nothing seems worthwhile,
When hour by hour the minutes drag
  And each step seems a mile.

There comes a time in every life
  So like a minor chord
But that's not the time to lose your faith
  It's the time to use it for the Lord.

There comes a time in every life
  When none can give you aid
But He who lives and reigns above
  For that's how we are made.

There comes a time in every life
  When God is all in all;
No human hand, no voice, no tear
  Can quite satisfy your call.

And if that certain time is yours
  To face this very night,
God grant you peace and faith and hope
  Until tomorrow's light.

If we suffer, we shall also reign with him. . . .

2 Timothy 2:12

Gethsemane

We each have our own Gethsemane
   A cross that we must bear,
A bitter cup that we must drink,
   But God is with us there.

Beyond the realm of time and tide
   We'll know the why and how;
God sees much more than we can see
   And that's enough for now.

Trust in the Lord with all your heart
and lean not on your own understanding.

Proverbs 3:5 NIV

TRUST

. . . thou anointest my head with oil;
my cup runneth over.

Psalms 23:5

Like a Tree

The breeze blows the trees
    and the leaves know not why;
They move at the slightest
    command;
They trust in their branches
    to hold them secure
Like the Father holds us
    in His hand.

Each tree has its roots
    planted firm in the soil;
Each leaf knows the source
    of its life;
By faith it holds fast
    come sun or come rain
As we cling to God
    through earth's strife.

We, too, know the source
    of our hope and our strength—
The Master who measures
    each season;
We, too, trust His wisdom,
    His mercy, His love;
We know if skies cloud—
    there's a reason.

He shall be like a tree planted by the rivers of water, that bringeth forth his fruit in his season. . . .

Psalms 1:3

A Little Rest

A little rest with time to think
   Is sometimes what God wills;
A time to gather faith and strength
   To climb life's rugged hills.

So let your heart and mind be filled
   With thoughts of peace and love;
Make this a time to calmly wait
   And trust the One above.

And after you have suffered a little while, the God of all grace, who has called you to his eternal glory in Christ, will himself restore, establish, and strengthen you.

1 Peter 5:10 RSV

Trust in Him

God never forsakes His own, I know,
    He will not leave me now;
No matter how hard may be the test,
    He'll see me through somehow.

Oh, why should I question God's own way
    If steep my path should be?
I know though it leads me to a cross,
    Still, still my God loves me.

Oh, why should I fear earth's mountain heights
    Nor yet death's grave below
For God is my strength, my hope, my shield,
    I know, I know, I know.

My times are in thy hand. . . .

Psalms 31:15

I'm Safe

I can't see the wind and I can't see love
But I know for sure when it's there;
I can't see faith and I can't see God,
But I know I'm safe in His care.

It's Sufficient

I know God made in His own time
   Both man and land and sea:
I know God is, I know I'm His
   And His grace is sufficient for me.

*My grace is sufficient for you, for my power is made
perfect in weakness. . . .*

2 Corinthians 12:9 NIV

Let Go and Let God

Let go and let God
decide
what is best;
Trust in His love,
in Him
sweetly rest.
Though waters may cover
the sea
and the land,
They rise or divide
by the touch
of His hand;
Though mountains grow rugged
and valleys
grow deep,
Just walk with the Lord,
your watch
He will keep.

Let the sky that's above you
be cloudy
and gray,
He has a purpose
so give Him
His way.
Let go and let God
decide
what is best;
Trust in His love,
in Him
sweetly rest.

But blessed is the man who trusts in the Lord. . . .

Jeremiah 17:7 NIV

The Way of a Rose

I'm sure the rose that sweetly grows
    Along the garden wall
Thinks not of tears beyond the wall
    Or petals that may fall.
It lifts its face to God above
    Serenely day by day
And questions not, if it should rain,
    The wisdom of God's way.
I'm sure the rose that sweetly grows
    Has burdens just as I;
The weather's far too wet, too cold,
    And yet it asks not why.

Then how much more should I trust God
    When days are dark and drear;
Then how much more should I give thanks
    That God is always near?
Then how much more should I believe
    God understands—He knows?
Then how much more should I trust God?
    Am I . . . less than a rose?

. . . He is my refuge and my fortress: my God; in him will I trust.

Psalms 91:2

Not What It Seems

What seems to be a stumbling block
   May be a stepping-stone;
What seems to be a solid wall
   May be a door unknown;
What seems to be a speck of dust
   May be, in truth, pure gold;
So walk by faith and not by sight,
   No good will God withhold.

All Is Well

Tomorrow is here
the day
I feared
yesterday
and God is still
in control
and always will
be.

For the Lord God is a sun and shield: the Lord will give grace and glory: no good thing will he withhold from them that walk uprightly.

Psalms 84:11

HOPE

Surely goodness and mercy shall follow me all the days of my life. . . .

Psalms 23:6

He Cares

I know that I can trust the Lord
   To keep the stars in place,
To grant the lark, the rose, the oak
   His wisdom and His grace.

I know that I can trust the Lord
   To send the morning light,
To turn each winter into spring,
   To rule each depth, each height.

I know that everywhere I look
   I see His guiding hand,
More beauty, mercy, love and faith
   Than I can understand.

Then why should I refuse to trust
   Those things I cannot see
To Him who knows tomorrow's needs?
   He cares for you and me.

*So don't be anxious about tomorrow. God will take care of
your tomorrow too. Live one day at a time.*

Matthew 6:34 TLB

New Day

Hearts sometimes seem to hold within
    A hurricane of grief,
A storm of highest magnitude,
    Doubt wrestles with belief.

But peace will come through shattered
      dreams
    If we but wait and pray;
God holds within His mighty hand
    A new and brighter day.

As Time Goes By

Great disappointments often come
When such are least expected;
We feel that life has been in vain,
We feel alone, neglected.
But just beyond the bend ahead
Lies treasure all unknown;
God sees it there and it shall be
Yours, too, when faith has grown.
So trust His wisdom all the way
And never ask Him why;
You'll find true peace of mind, true
hope
Will come as time goes by.

*Now the God of hope fill you with all joy and peace . . . that
ye may abound in hope. . . .*

Romans 15:13

Hope's Miracle

Hope
is faith's rainbow,
the promise of
spring,
a giving, living,
beautiful thing
that can grow
till some bright tomorrow
we'll know
a miracle
has happened in
God's very special way.
So—
hold on, *hope* on and
pray.

. . . hope we have as an anchor of the soul, both sure and stedfast. . . .

Hebrews 6:19

Hope's Song

Hope is such a fragile, gossamer thing;
It comes and it goes like showers
    in spring.

And yet, it's true we all need it so;
I know, I know, ah yes, I know.

Without it life's nothing, it's
    nothing at all,
For every tomorrow is a high stone wall.

A wall that has in it no stairs and no door,
Nothing but wall, solid wall, and no more.

There's only one way to hold on to hope;
There's only one way one can really cope.

Faith is the answer, faith is the way;
Faith in our Father each night and each day.

Hope is such a fragile, gossamer thing,
But hope has a long, happy song faith
    can sing.

. . . whoso trusteth in the Lord, happy is he.

Proverbs 16:20

Hope

Hope is a stranger
    if it lacks faith and love,
a beggar who knocks at
    your door;
Hope is a table without any
    bread,
a pitcher that
    refuses to
    pour.

But hope is
    a garden where
    little dreams grow,
the bud of
    a beautiful flower;
Rooted in faith and
    nurtured by love
    it has
    God given, soul healing
    power.

And now these three remain: faith, hope and love. . . .

1 Corinthians 13:13 NIV

PROMISE

*. . . and I will dwell in the house of the Lord
for ever.*

Psalms 23:6

Across the Great Divide

When I put out to sail the sea
   Across the great divide,
My heart shall have no fear, no dread
   For I have faith inside.

I know I shall not sail alone
   Nor shall I lose the way;
My Pilot shall be with me then
   Just as He is today.

When I put out to sail the sea,
   Let faith fill your heart, too,
For somewhere on that other shore
   I'll watch and wait—for you.

He that believeth on the Son hath everlasting life. . . .

John 3:36

Autumn Leaf

The falling leaves remind me that
   I, too, shall change some day;
I'll leave behind my frail abode
   Of earthly dust and clay.

I somehow think God lets leaf souls
   Emerge just like my own;
Transformed, they're never wholly "gone"
   Just freed to some unknown.

Like them I'll don a bright new robe
   And join the heavenly band
Some day when my own autumn comes—
   A leaf at God's command.

. . . because I live, ye shall live also.

John 14:19

Safe

If roses are but twice as fair
   when washed by heaven's dew;
If robin's song is twice as sweet
   and skies are twice as blue;
If love and life are twice as grand
   as all we feel and see,
How marvelous! How wonderful
   must all God's heaven be!

Then why should we give way to tears?
   All grief and pain is past;
Our loved one's safe from every harm,
   Safe—home . . . at last.

*Come unto me, all ye that labour and are heavy laden,
and I will give you rest.*

Matthew 11:28

90

God's Garden

God works in His garden,
I'm told every day
With the roses He needs
for His heavenly bouquet.
There are times when He picks
all the withered, the old,
And gathers them lovingly
into His fold.
There are times when He prunes
where some other must grow
That He on the weak ones
more strength may bestow.
But some days He chooses
the fairest in sight;
He needs certain buds
to make heaven look bright.
How sweet, oh, how beautiful
is His bouquet!
God works in His garden
and best is His way.

To every thing there is a season, and a time to every purpose. . . .

Ecclesiastes 3:1

Some Bright Tomorrow

Though trials surround me,
    all things are well,
I'll trust in Jesus,
    His love I'll tell;
Nor will I question
    the way He planned,
Some bright tomorrow
    I'll understand.

Tears shall be ended,
    all pain shall cease,
When I see Jesus
    I'll find sweet peace;
There'll be no sorrow,
    this God has planned;
Some bright tomorrow
    I'll understand.

I'm looking forward
    to that bright day
When I shall vacate
    this house of clay;
I'll live with Jesus
    eternally;
Some bright tomorrow
    His face I'll see.

Some bright tomorrow
    I'll understand,
Some bright tomorrow
    in God's fair land;
I'll see and know Him,
    I'll touch His hand!
Some bright tomorrow
    I'll understand.

And whosoever liveth and believeth in me shall never die. . . .

John 11:26